Cambodia Refugees
In Long Beach, California
The Definitive Study

Scott Shaw

Buddha Rose Publications

Library of Congress
Cataloging in Publication Data
Cambodian Refugees in Long Beach, California
1. Khmer-California-Long Beach.
2. Refugees-California-Long Beach.
3. Long Beach (Calif.)-Social conditions. I. Title
F869.L7S53 1989 305.8'9593079493 89-22148

ISBN 1-877792-02-0
ISBN-13: 978-1877792021

Library of Congress Catalog Card Number
89-81898

10 9 8 7 6 5 4 3 2 1
Printed in the United States of America

Cambodia Refugees
In Long Beach, California
The Definitive Study

Contents

Introduction   **7**

Chapter 1   **9**
Cambodia's Historical Background

Chapter 2   **17**
The First Movement of Refugees

Chapter 3   **23**
**Demographics, Population,
    and the People of the
    Cambodia Section
    of Long Beach, California**

Chapter 4   **33**
Housing Among Cambodia Refugees

   Photographs of Housing   **39**

Chapter 5   **43**
Education Among Cambodia Refugees

Chapter 6   **51**
**Employment Trends of Cambodians
    in Long Beach, California**

   Photographs of Businesses   **61**

Chapter 7   **71**
**The Politics of Cambodia Refugees
    in Long Beach, California**

Chapter 8   **79**
**Cambodia Assimilation
    of American Culture**

Chapter 9   **87**
Survey

Chapter 10   **89**
Sample Survey

Chapter 11   **95**
Survey Results 1986

Chapter 12   **107**
Survey Results 1989

    Survey Illustrations   **119**

Conclusion   **135**

References   **137**

About the Author   **143**

Scott Shaw's Books-In-Print   **145**

Introduction

Cambodia has been in a state of political and cultural conflict for the past three decades. This was epitomized by the political reign of terror brought on by Pol Pot, the leader of the Khmer Rouge, as he seized power in 1975. His attempt to create a completely agrarian society left the country in chaos and an estimated three million Cambodians dead.

Since that time, Cambodians began to seek sanctuary in less hostile environments. With this, many left their native land and entered the United States as refugees. This movement to America has had one city as a focal point: Long Beach, California. To date, there are an estimated thirty-five thousand Cambodians living there.

The majority of the Cambodians, who have come to Long Beach, have arrived directly from refugee camps in Thailand. They have come in a pre-literate state with virtually no finances or possessions. Once in the city, they have begun to be supported by state aid. Feeling quite alien to western culture, they have developed a dependency for this aid which few have made an attempt to move away from and onto self-reliance.

The City of Long Beach is left with a new and continually growing ethnic group, who are supported by the government, live in overcrowded, unsanitary conditions and make little or no attempt at American assimilation.

This study will not attempt to chronicle the war in Southeast Asia or Cambodia for this has been done extensively in the past. This text will view where the majority of Cambodians who have left their homeland have relocated to: Long Beach, California. It will evaluate their life style there and the factors that have contributed to it.

As an aid to drawing conclusions for this study, two surveys were conducted: the first one of one hundred Cambodian inhabitants of this area in August of 1986, the second one was taken of one thousand Cambodian Refugees, completed in June of 1989. This study will hope to conclude the effect and impact this movement has had on both the City of Long Beach and the Cambodians, who have located there.

Chapter 1

Cambodia's Historical Background

Cambodia has been inhabited since the Neolithic Period. This is documented by archaeological findings. The recorded history of Cambodia dates back to the First Century A.D. Its history can roughly be divided into five distinct periods. The first—that of the kingdoms of Fu-nan and Chen-la, existed from the beginning of the Christian era to the end of the Eighth Century AD. This period was followed by the Kambuja or Ankgor period which lasted until the early 1400`s. Cambodia then entered a period of decline, struggling for existence. The country was virtually consumed by neighboring Thailand and Vietnam. This period finally came to a close in 1864 when Cambodia became a French protectorate. The final period, which exists today, may be called the modern period, which extends from the independence of Cambodia from the French through the recent Southeast Asian War, until present day, where Vietnam, the power which held political control over Cambodia since the fall of the Khmer Rouge regime is currently removing its military forces.

The first inhabitants of Cambodia are said to have lived in the area of the Mekong River and Delta. Here, life and food sources were abundant. There were three distinct politically independent ethnic groups that lived in this region: the Funanese, the Chams, and the Khmer—the ancestors of the present dominate racial stock, which inhabit Cambodia today.

The Fu-nan period (A.D. 200-535) was controlled by the Funanese. By the end of the Third Century, this group had control of the entire Mekong area. Fu-nan was an expansionist country, attacking and conquering the neighboring kingdoms until the end of the Fifth Century.

According to Chinese documents an Indian Brahman ruled the kingdom for a time and its customs became Indianized. The Indian social structure was put into practice, as was the Sanskrit alphabet. Today a modified version of the alphabet is still in use.

Fu-nan fell into decline in the middle of the Sixth Century. It was seceded by one of its then vassal states, Chen-la. The Chen-la period lasted between AD 535-802.

During the two hundred and fifty years Chen-la was dominant, it extended its empire to the boundaries of present day China. Chen-la was finally subdued by internal strife.

The name, "Cambodia," derives from the Chen-la period. Chen-la was inhabited predominately by Khmer people, whose legendary founder was Kambu Svayambhuva, hence the French, "Kambuja," and the English, "Cambodia."

The Kambuja or Ankgor period (A.D. 8021432) is considered Cambodia's period of greatness. At its peak this kingdom extended from the Annam chain of mountains, in present day Vietnam, to the Gulf of Siam. During this period not only were the greatest structures in Cambodian history built, Angkor Wat and the Bayon of Angkor Thom, but also the people were prosperous, arts flourished and according to Chinese records, hospitals and extensive irrigation existed.

The Khmer became the source of continual and increasing attacks both from Siam, now Thailand and Annaim, present day Vietnam. These continued attacks eventually brought about the decline of Angkor and the Khmer people. This period lasted between 1432 and 1864. Their kingdom became a small virtually non-existent country dominated by Thailand, who continually tried to enforce its claimed sovereignty over the country by forceful means.

Both Thailand and Vietnam claimed territories. Due to continual defeats in battle, the political boundaries of the country became quite small.

Cambodia tried to enlist the help of the Spanish as a means of saving its challenged independence, but when the first military expedition was wiped out, Spain lost interest. It was not until 1863 when Cambodia became a French ally that the tides began to turn.

In April of 1864, Cambodia became a French protectorate. Under the control of a foreign government, they became secure against the invasions of Thailand and Vietnam. France had complete control of most areas of the Cambodian government, and by 1884 Cambodia had become virtually a colony of France. Internal opposition against France's domination resulted in a two-year uprising. In 1887, France formed the Union of Indochina, giving the local governments more political control, causing the resistance on the part of Cambodians to diminish greatly.

The Japanese occupied Cambodia briefly during World War II but French control returned in 1945. At this time the country was made a member of the French Union. In 1953, the country gained independence from France and was completely in control of its political affairs.

The first leader of the independent Cambodia was Prince Norodom Sihanouk. He was born into the family of the King of Cambodia, 31 October 1922. The French had helped him gain the throne in 1941, but in 1955 he abdicated in favor of his father. He then went on to politics, and in 1955, the political group he had formed won every seat in the Cambodian National Assembly and he was appointed Prime Minister, a position he kept until 1970.

The Vietnam War was in full swing by the late 1960's. Prince Sihanouk's government by this time was also beginning to have problems for there was a rising amount of protest against his leadership due to enormous corruption. This, combined with the Vietcong using the Southern reaches of the country for havens, put the once neutral country in a precarious position of which it has never been able to recover.

On 18 March 1970, a coup was launched against the Sihanouk government and Prince Norodom

Sihanouk was overthrown. He left the country and entered China. On 30 April 1970, President Nixon announced that American and South Vietnamese troops had entered the country militarily. In October of that same year, the new Prime Minister Lon Nol proclaimed that Cambodia was now to be known as the Khmer Republic or Kampuchea.

Lon Nol was born 13 November 1913, and died a resident of Fullerton, California, 17 November 1985. He was in control of Cambodia from the overthrow of Prince Sihanouk in 1970 until 1975. With the help of the United States, his attempt to eliminate the communist influence in Cambodia led to a civil war. In May of 1975, the communist Khmer Rouge forces defeated Lon Nol's army and captured the Cambodian capital city of Phnom Pehn.

Pol Pot and Khieu Samphan were leaders of the Khmer Rouge and succeeded Lon Nol as the heads of Cambodia. Pol Pot became the Prime Minister and Khieu Samphan, who had received a Ph.D. in economics from the University of Paris in 1959, became the Head of State.

Prime Minister Pol Pot, in his attempt to build an entirely agrarian based society, forced the immediate evacuation of all the urban centers of Cambodia and placed all the people into cruel farm orientated work camps. All those with any education, position, or even those who wore glasses were considered corrupt and unworthy. These work camps and the governmental practices are believed to have killed up to three million people in the few years the Khmer Rouge was in power. People are reported to have died through starvation, beatings, and torture. In January of 1979, the Vietnamese government overthrew Pol Pot, Khieu Samphan, and their party.

The scene today in Cambodia is not as bleak as it was pre-1979. Due to the Vietnamese occupation, the cities have been repopulated and there is no longer forced labor and starvation as there once was.

The world community did not appreciate the political occupation of Cambodia, nor by indigenous population, who were unhappy with their inability to govern themselves. Through continued negotiation, the Vietnamese military occupation ended in 1989. The geographical region and country, which had been most recently known as Kampuchea, has now returned to the name of Cambodia.

The removal of the very strong Vietnamese military has left the country in a very precarious situation due to the fact that all of the politically interested parties have been unable to reach an agreement as to who should lead Cambodia. It is now believed that the country will continue into another period of civil unrest because of the lack of political direction and it has concerned the world that the Khmer Rouge, who are still militarily active in the region, may return to power.

Chapter 2
The First Movement of Refugees

The first mass movement of Cambodians out of their native land came as a result of the Khmer Rouge victory over the government of Lon Nol in 1975.

Cambodians began fleeing their country even before the end of the war, which was to leave the Khmer Rouge in power on 17 April 1975. The majority of the first group of refugees crossed the Thai border and, being relatively small in numbers, was not of concern to the Thai government.

This first group of refugees was, for the most part, educated and affluent urban dwellers that saw the implications of what was to come with the new regime in power. Many of these people found it easy to claim refugee status and quickly immigrate to the United States. Others founded the first refugee camp in Thailand at the temple, Wat Koh. Since the Thai government did not consider this movement of refugees into their border a problem in the beginning, these Cambodians were allowed to move freely within this area, some obtaining jobs while many, within a short time, obtained a way to relocate to a western country.

The United States defines an acceptable refugee as someone who is leaving their country due to political pressures that are adverse to the person and the United States government. A prospective refugee who hopes to relocate in the United States must also be confirmed to have not partaken in or been accomplice to the actions of the government which has seized power. In other words, one cannot hope to come to the United States if they have been in any way, officially or unofficially, connected to the government they are fleeing or have committed deeds that the United States does not deem worthy. As for the first group of refugees this was not a problem. It was later much more difficult to define what alliances a Cambodian may have had.

As time progressed, those wishing to leave the reign of terror that the new Pol Pot, Khmer Rouge government was instating, flooded the Thai-Cambodian border. It was belittling the educated, the wealthy, the accomplished and forcing them all to become peasant laborers. Thailand did not expect this occurrence nor were they willing or prepared to deal with it. This, the problem for Thailand and the Cambodian Refugees began.

The formation of refugee camps was frowned upon by Thailand as early as 1976, when the government began to see its implications. No longer were those fleeing the Cambodian government simply well to do, educated urbanites that could be expected to finance their own resettlement and blend into Thai society or quickly relocate to the United States. More and more peasant farmers, fishermen, and laborers were fleeing the new government, as well.

Cambodian Refugees were becoming the focal point of the world. Organizations such as the Red Cross, UNICEF, and the United Nations were beginning to enter the picture and come to the aid of the newly arrived refugees. By June of 1979, there were over forty thousand Cambodians amassed along the Thai-Cambodian border. The majority of these people had hopes of relocating to other countries and using Thailand as their stopping point en route.

The strain this began to put on Thailand was obvious. Aid from foreign nations was slow in coming. It was not until 24 October 1979, that then President Carter pledged thirty million dollars for the first six months of international relief efforts in

Cambodia and nine million for Khmers who had fled their government into Thailand.

The Thai government and its corrupt army and police officials saw the financial possibilities of this new movement of people into the expanding amount of refugee camps within Thai borders. These military personnel began forcing the incoming Cambodians to literally pay to enter the borders and the camps. Once inside the camps, the refugees were often forced to pay for services.

Of all the refugees in Long Beach interviewed for this study who were in these camps, all were required to pay for entrance through the border and into the Thai refugee camps. These refugees would make their payments in pieces of gold they had or in United States currency they may have had the opportunity of obtaining and so on.

With the fall of the Khmer Rouge government and the occupation of Cambodia by Vietnam in 1979, the problem of refugees intensified. At this juncture, not only were refugee camps set up in Thailand, but they were also in existence along the Cambodian side of the border. These camps, under the control of the Khmer Rouge and other Cambodian groups opposed to the Vietnamese occupation of Cambodia, had and have thousands of inhabitants who were fleeing not only political and social conditions, but the Vietnamese as well.

For those Cambodians who wished to remain in their country but simply not support the Vietnamese occupation, they located themselves in these camps ruled often times unsparingly by the Khmer Rouge. Not only were these camps not as well organized as those on the Thailand side of the border but also they were often the targets of Vietnamese shelling. At these times the people flee, crossing the border into Thailand. This, of course, puts more strain on the region and Thailand.

For those who entered Thailand post 1979 and wished to come to America, the decision was a difficult one for the United States to make. It was necessary to screen out any former Khmer Rouge officials and supporters since these people would not be allowed into the United States under normal refugee standards. Yet, it is claimed by many relocated Cambodians that, in fact, Khmer Rouge sympathizers and officials have entered the United States. Many of the latter arriving Cambodian Refugees found it difficult to obtain an easy and quick means to the United States.

As of July 1986, the United States government believed that it had done its part in aiding Cambodian Refugees in terms of granting refugee asylum; having admitted more than five hundred thousand Indo-Chinese Refugees, it was believed that the majority of those eligible under refugee status have been processed. Though the border areas of Cambodia and Thailand are still in the midst of conflict and Cambodians continually petition to enter the United States, it is felt that all those now applying were at least supporters of the Khmer Rouge government. The alternative for those still at the border camps and wishing to come to America is to obtain permission in other ways. This may generally be accomplished if one has relatives now residing in the United States or is able to obtain a sponsor.

The decision to stop general admission of Cambodian Refugees is highly debated by all people and governments concerned. The United States government believes that it cannot have a one hundred percent acceptance policy or the country would be overrun by all those wishing to immigrate.

Chapter 3

Demographics, Population, and the People of the Cambodian Section of Long Beach, California

California State University, Long Beach, during the 1960's, hosted approximately one hundred exchange students from Cambodia. While attending the university, Cambodian students formed the Cambodian Student Association. This organization continued through the sixties as a means of helping new Cambodian students, who had arrived at the school. Few of these students chose to remain in America; most preferred to return to their country and help with the knowledge they had acquired in the United States. As the political climate of Southeast Asia changed and Cambodia became involved, many of those who had attended the university chose to return to the United States in hope of a more peaceful life. Along with these people came others, who wished to escape the decaying political condition of Cambodia.

From this movement, the Long Beach Cambodian community was born.

With the continual rise in the number of Cambodians moving to the United States, the former students and early Cambodian immigrants renamed and reformed the Cambodian Student Association, to the Cambodian Association of America in an effort to help the Cambodians in their transition to American life.

The majority of Cambodians, who have had the opportunity of coming to the United States, have, for the most part, tried to make Long Beach, California their home. Here they have been able to not only find a forming community, but economic and educational aid as well.

The movement of Cambodians to Long Beach has been a relatively recent occurrence. In 1975, one finds that there were only seven Cambodian families residing in Long Beach. Since 1975, literally thousands of Cambodian Refugees have come each year. In 1981, over four thousand relocated to the City of Long Beach. Today there are no actual figures for the amount of Cambodians that are in the city, but it is estimated to be between thirty-five thousand and fifty thousand.

The area of Long Beach where the majority of Cambodians live is bound roughly by Pacific Coast Highway to the east, Seventh Street to the west, Long Beach Boulevard to the north, and Redondo Avenue to the south.

Within these boundaries, one finds the condition of the housing to be in disrepair and the living conditions overcrowded. Never-the-less, Cambodians still wish to make the move to this area. They have arrived from a country, which had decaying conditions, both politically and socially. To them Long Beach is a haven and is by far better than the conditions they left behind in Cambodia.

The City of Long Beach considers the Cambodian area to be a low-income, predominantly black section. It has however, as of 1987, begun to see the impending problem that is looming with the continual flow of Cambodians into the already overcrowded and unsanitary living conditions.

The United States Census has also overlooked this area in terms of its actual population make up and density. It describes the area as 36.9 percent white, 18.5 percent black, .7 percent American Indian, 4.9 percent Asian, 14.6 percent unspecified, and 24.4 percent Hispanic. This may be a rough view of the racial make-up of the area but it does not take into consideration the amount of undeclared Cambodians that currently inhabit the area. The total reported population of the neighborhood is forty-six thousand, seven hundred and ninety-eight (46,798). This definitely does not take into consideration the estimated thirty-five thousand to fifty thousand Cambodians who are believed to reside there. Perhaps with the upcoming 1990 Census, a more definitive assessment of this area may be concluded.

The population trends of Cambodians moving to this area of Long Beach will undoubtedly continue. This is especially true because of the fact that so many newly arrived Cambodian Refugees, who are initially located in other regions, move to Long Beach. There is no way for the government to control this movement.

Refuges who could not finance their own move to America or found difficulties in coming here were often helped by generous American sponsors, who provided financial guarantees as well as transportation for their arrivals to the United States. The Cambodians, anxious to arrive here, were not concerned with particulars and accepted any stipulation presented. It is estimated that the majority of the thirty percent of Cambodians, who are Christians converted in the refugee camps in order to obtain sponsors, leaving the traditional religion of their country Theravana Buddhism. The refugees being only interested in leaving the troubled region were not concerned with where they were relocated to in the United States. Once in America however, upon hearing of the community in Long Beach, the refugees left the care of their sponsors, relocated, and began to collect local financial aid. This process is not only unfortunate for the sponsors, but it also places an enormous burden on the State of California.

There has only been one noticeable exception to this flow of continuum to Long Beach that occurred when the 1 October 1987 earthquake struck the Los Angeles area. The majority of Cambodians had never experienced an earthquake of any magnitude. With the earthquake, the ensuing concern of a larger upcoming quake, and superstitions the Cambodian's traditionally hold, approximately four to five hundred families moved from the Long Beach area to Southeast Asian refugee communities in the California central valley; namely in: Fresno, Stockton, and Modesto. This however, is a small fraction of the remaining Cambodian population and the influx of new families that continue to move into this geographic vicinity.

The Cambodian agencies that are located in Long Beach make no judgment of a Cambodian move to the Long Beach community. They feel it is their position to simply help the Cambodians find a way to survive in America, which usually involves welfare. Within the boundaries of the Cambodian community, there are no actual figures as to the amount of Cambodians that live on welfare, but it is estimated that at least eight percent of the Cambodians located there are supported by it.

The city scene is not a pretty one. Buildings are old, overcrowded, and this vicinity claims the highest crime rate in Long Beach. 57.7 percent of the residences live below the economic poverty level, making below ten thousand dollars a year. The United States Census claims that sixteen thousand, seven hundred and ninety-three (16,793) of the total forty-six thousand, seven hundred ninety-eight (46,798) people who inhabit this area of Long Beach live in overcrowded conditions. The City of Long Beach estimates it to be slightly more, but they have no actual figures and rely on that of the government's figures. The fact is that these numbers are completely incorrect in both amounts and proportions. It only takes a simple view into the community or a look inside some of the apartment complexes to ascertain this.

The City of Long Beach realizing the impending problem claims that corrective measures are now being taken. If, in fact, corrective measures are underway, this will undoubtedly solve the surface of the problem, but only for a short time; for if the Cambodians began to feel threatened, they will simply become more shrouded in their already concealing living situations.

Is there an absolute answer for the population problem that is in existence in the Cambodian community of Long Beach? The only solution that would cause mass exodus would be if Cambodia were returned to a democratic or at least tolerable government. With this the majority of the Cambodian Refugees would return to their native land. Aside from this, there are no answers. All who attempt a solution are speaking simply in philosophic terms. As long as Cambodian Refugees continue to leave Cambodia and find a road to America, either through relatives or sponsorship, the number of Cambodian residences, living in this community will multiply and the boundaries will grow.

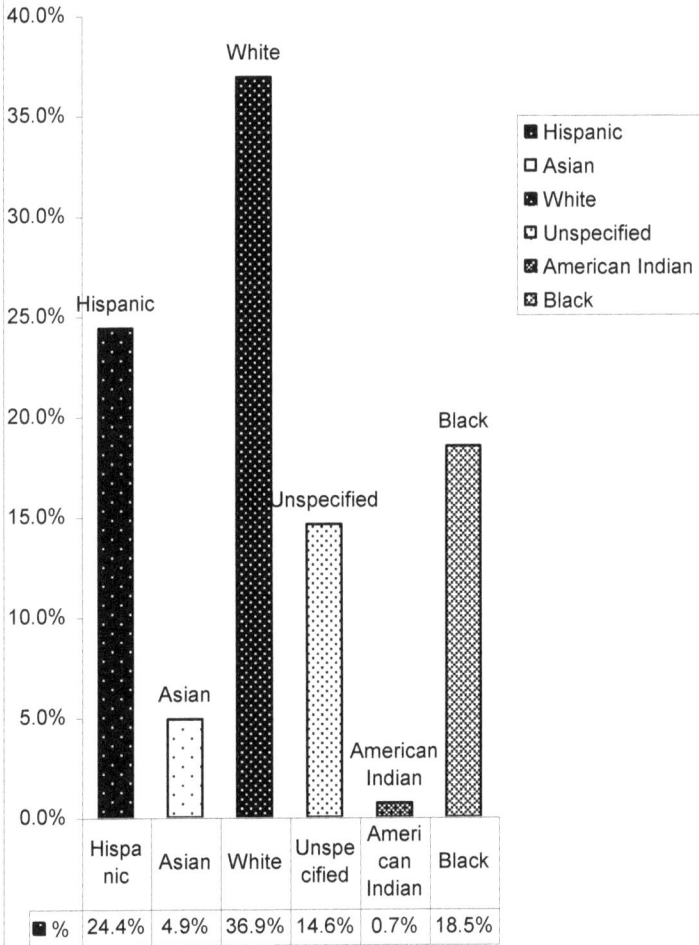

Illustration 1
Population Percentages
1986 U.S. Census Update

Legend:
- Hispanic
- Asian
- White
- Unspecified
- American Indian
- Black

	Hispanic	Asian	White	Unspecified	American Indian	Black
%	24.4%	4.9%	36.9%	14.6%	0.7%	18.5%

Chapter 4

Housing Among Cambodia Refugees

The housing profile of the Cambodian area of Long Beach is similar to that of other low-income areas of the United States. Within these boundaries we find that the average home is valued at $56,973.00, according to the 1989 United States Census update. Local real estate agents place the figure at more probably $85,000.00, which is still a low home-value figure. In fact, this is not only a low value for a home in California but is especially the case when the home is located within such a close proximity to the Pacific Ocean. The home value price of this area leads one to the obvious conclusion of the age and condition of the housing that make up the area.

Over thirty percent of the housing units were constructed prior to 1940. Since that time the amount of structures built each year has continued to decline. Along with this decline has also come a deterioration of twenty years. Since old and dilapidated city ridden and new ethnic minorities can dwell with little or no external judgment, this area of Long Beach has served its purpose well, for it has provided a suitable location for the newly arrived Cambodian Refugees to form a community.

There are a total of fifteen thousand, seven hundred seventy-nine (15,779) housing units, which roughly comprise the defined Cambodian area. Of these total units, the owners occupy only 14.7 percent. Renters, therefore, are the predominate occupants. These renters make up eighty-six percent of those who live in the Cambodian area of Long Beach. Here one finds that the average rent is $228.00 per month. This also obviously reflects the condition of the housing, for the housing units, both single-family homes and apartment buildings, are predominantly old and uncared for.

As of early 1989, there were a total of nine hundred ninety-one units for sale or rent in this area. This is 6.3 percent of the total number of living structures that make up the entire area. Of this 6.3 percent, almost ninety percent were for rent, not for sale. What one may conclude from this is that not only do owners hold on to their properties, undoubtedly to have rental income, but also that the people who rent these dwellings rarely move, obviously due to the economic and social conditions.

According to the 1986 update of the United States Census, sixteen thousand, seven hundred ninety-three (16,793) of the total forty-six thousand, seven hundred ninety-eight (46,798) people that make up this area live in overcrowded conditions. Though this figure, as in all ghetto situations, is misleading due to the fact that low-income housing dwellers rarely reveal the actual amount of people living under one roof—it does, none-the-less, give one a general understanding of the way the people who make up this area live. These figures state that roughly one third of the structures are overcrowded.

Cambodians, on the whole, are not averse to living with several families within one dwelling or one large family in a very small dwelling. As the findings of the survey conducted for this study are analyzed, what is found is that over half of those interviewed lived in apartments and of those who did, all the apartments would be considered overcrowded by the standard formula of two persons to each room of a living structure. Of those that lived in single-family units or homes, the majority of the houses would be considered overcrowded as well.

Entering overcrowded apartments occupied by Cambodian Refugees, one finds such things as make-shift walls constructed from sheets and tables used for eating during the day and sleeping under at night. Insects and pests are also quite common in this old section of Long Beach. Since many Cambodians are not up to the hygienic standards practiced here in the United States, these insects have a free breeding ground and are often seen on walls and on the furniture.

The environments of those living in overcrowded single-family structures are not much different. With this vast amount of formerly peasant farmers moving into seemingly modern structures also comes a large amount of structural decay. This is not due so much to the uncleanliness of these people, but simply due to a different set of standards and definition of what is acceptable.

Of the Cambodian owned businesses that lie within the boundaries, those who own the business, in many cases, live in the structures in which their businesses are located. This is obviously against city code, and so the City of Long Beach has begun to take action against these code infractions. This action, by its very nature, is a hard move to follow through with, for not only will these business dwellers become more secretive, but will be better concealed as well.

The reason that the City of Long Beach needs to take action against these people who live at their businesses is that the majority of these businesses are food services, namely: restaurants and grocery stores. This is obviously a health hazard to all who frequent these establishments. In these cases the ability to spread disease is quite prevalent.

The Cambodians are at least seemingly satisfied with their living conditions. They are a family orientated people who remain in close ties. America has undoubtedly altered this family structure at least to some degree, especially among the ones who came here at an early age and have become more akin to and influenced by American culture. Yet, as demonstrated by the surveys, the majority wishes to remain living with their families. What also may be noted is that the majority of those interviewed are more or less content with their living situation.

There are two notable differences within the findings of the surveys in regards to housing. One is that all those Cambodians, who are now attending college and have a good command of the language and culture of America, desire not only to move to a better living space but also feel that eventually they will move away from their immediate families. These facts are undoubtedly contributed to by the length of time spent assimilating American culture and values. As to whether one may see this as a breakdown of Cambodian morals and culture, it is an academic issue. For whether or not this is the case remains unimportant; simply that some of the people of this community are striving for higher living standards gives the area hope of improvement.

Cambodian Refugees, on the whole, came from very poor living conditions in their native Cambodia. The housing structures of Long Beach are a vast improvement from what most had known in their homeland. To an American eye, they seem unlivable due to the overcrowding, structural condition, and poor-hygienics. Yet, to a Cambodian, it is undoubtedly a vast improvement over the refugee camps and the archaic conditions of Cambodia.

Photographs of Housing
in the Cambodian Section of Long Beach, California, circa 1987

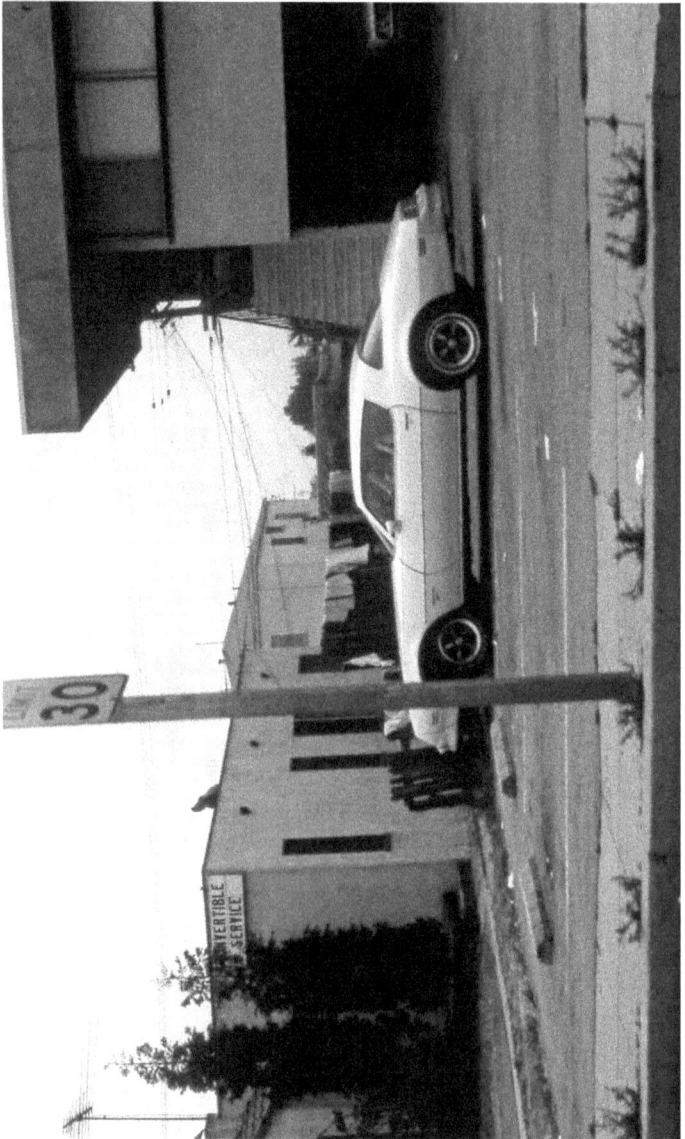

Chapter 5
Education Among Cambodian Refugees

Education is the basis in which any interaction on the cultural, social, or economic level is based. That level of education, or lack of it, is also the foundation for which a newly arrived minority group, such as the Cambodians, makes their way into the mainstream of the society of which they have become a part; in this case, American society.

As mentioned earlier, the first Cambodian contact with the United States came through Cambodian students attending California State University, Long Beach. This correlation with a university is almost ironic when one views the educational standards of the adult Cambodians who have arrived since 1979. Over sixty-eight percent have less than eight years of education and twenty-two percent have never attended school. This lack of education has set the climate for a current situation that now exists in the Cambodian community of Long Beach.

There is no value judgment to be made of the Cambodians who have arrived, virtually education less, in the more recent past. Over seventy-five percent of these people were rural farmers or fishermen and they had not had the opportunity or even the need to develop the ability of reading and writing. Their society was structured as such that they simply lived their lives as their ancestors had done for generations before them.

Education in Cambodia was for the elite. It was not available to the common man. This is where the difference between the Cambodian and Vietnamese society comes into play. The Vietnamese had many more years of direct French and American influence than did the Cambodians. To the Vietnamese, it was much more common to be educated, and in fact, expected. Cambodians, on the other hand, were not afforded this luxury by their government. This has left the majority of them, who have arrived in Long Beach, in a pre-literate state.

Of the Cambodians who have arrived since 1979, it is estimated that currently twenty percent of them have at least some ability in English, the rest have virtually none. As for those who arrived either during the 1975 exodus or before, it is believed that ninety percent are competent in at least the basics of the English language. This may be attributed to the fact that they were predominantly of the elite class of Cambodians, who were afforded an education. This, combined with the fact that they have now been living in this country for almost fifteen years, gives them the obvious educational edge.

When the second wave of Cambodians arrived, they were placed in a totally alien culture. Not only had few ever experienced any of the western technologies, but also ninety-five percent had never even heard the English language spoken.

After arriving in Long Beach, in order to collect welfare or state aid, the Cambodian Refugee is required to participate in what is known as the Refugee Development Program, (RDP). The RDP begins by training the new arrivals in English. This is, for the most part, much more of an attempt than an actual process. It is estimated by education officials that it takes the first seven weeks to even get the Cambodians to understand the use of a textbook.

One of the elementary problems that exist with RDP is that the State of California only allows funding for a person to study and become competent in the English Language in one year. In most cases, these Cambodians have arrived here pre-literate and have suffered years of malnutrition and mistreatment from their government. It is virtually impossible for them to have any command of the language in that amount of time.

The entire RDP program lasts a total of three years for a family, or one year and a half for a single person. In that time they are trained in English for one year and the remainder of the time in a job skill; a skill few will ever choose to put into practice, as will be discussed in the following chapter.

Long Beach City College is the institution where these refugees are educated and trained. Of the total refugee population that attends the RDP program eight-five to ninety percent are Cambodian. Of the newly arrived Cambodians, 99.9 percent enroll in this program. As previously mentioned, the welfare department requires this program, if one wishes to collect monetary aid.

The United States is by far one of the leading countries that help newly arrived immigrants. The question arises however, if this help is warranted and placed in the right direction. One finds that the programs themselves do not actually aid the unmotivated new comers to move forward and assimilate the new society of which they have become a part. They are simply allowed to play along, and as much frustration as they may feel, it is in no way the responsibility of the United States government. It is, however in fact, the duty of the newly arrived person to put all effort into self-reliance and to move away from the burdensome state of dependency that they have placed themselves into.

Can the Cambodian Refugees simply remain a burden on the City of Long Beach, the State of California, and the United States government is a highly debatable issue. It is clear that if life is much simpler in a state of dependency compared to that of independence, the prior will be chosen. Therefore, if the RDP wishes to be of worth at any level, it must reevaluate itself and see that under current standards it is not effective.

Of all those interviewed for this study over the age of twenty, all agreed that the program was not long enough, nor thorough enough. They all felt more educational time was needed especially in regards to obtaining any competency in English. With this higher command of the English language, all felt it would be a much easier transition into the work place.

As in all cases, the younger people have the ability to adapt and to change more readily than do adults. The refugee children go to public schools. Thus they have made a rapid adaptation to the customs and tongue of the local environment, and have become more accustomed to American education than have the adults.

The children of the first wave of Cambodian Refugees have had the opportunity to be here more than seven years. In that time they have continued through public schools, and some have gone on to the community college level. A few have gone on to the university level as well.

There are no actual figures of exactly how many Cambodians attend either public school or institutions of higher education. It is, however, believed that almost all Cambodians between the ages of five and thirteen are taking advantage of public education, and the majority of those between thirteen and eighteen are doing the same. As for those attending a community college after high school, the percentage is placed at about 30 percent. The number attending universities is believed to be small. It is understood that no newly arrived adult Cambodian has proceeded on from the RDP to the college or university level to date.

Of those Cambodian college students interviewed in the surveys in this study all had the interest of learning business and management skills. They hoped this would place them in a better position in the job market. Though they all felt subjects such as art, philosophy, and social science were important, they showed little interest in studying them.

The United States Census claims that of the Asians that live in the Cambodian area of Long Beach, four hundred and eight-eight (488) have attended elementary school, one hundred and fifty-four (154) have attended some high school, four hundred and twenty-four (424) have completed high school, three hundred and six (306) have gone to college, and three hundred and eleven (311) have completed college. These figures, though somewhat revealing, are quite inaccurate. The United States Census also claims an Asian population make-up of this area to be only two thousand, seven hundred and sixty-one (2,761). The fact is, however, that there are believed to be upwards of fifty thousand Cambodian Refugees living in this area alone.

The United States Census is not the only organization with unconfirmed or misleading facts. The state welfare department has no clear figures as to how many Cambodians they are aiding educationally or otherwise. Not only do these undocumented numbers give way to many miscalculations, but they also destroy hopes of proper understanding of the area.

As education is the building block for a functional human being in American society, one may come to the clear conclusion that with current practices the newly arrived and predominately illiterate Cambodians over the age of twenty have little hope of ever becoming a functional part of society. The only hope, from an educational standpoint, is the younger generation.

Chapter 6

Employment Trends of Cambodians in Long Beach, California

The Cambodians, who have arrived in the United States over the past three decades, have experienced what is known as culture shock. They have gone from a peaceful rural based country to one devastated by war and politics. Many of them then fleeing have come to a new land that lives at a technological level few ever dreamed existed.

The Cambodians who have come to Long Beach have obviously not had an easy road to assimilation and productivity. The ones who have obtained it have had to struggle quite hard. American society deems that a person who is worthy or independent must be able to financially take care of him or herself. For most Cambodian Refugees, this has not been easy to achieve.

The first group of Cambodians came to this country and to the Long Beach area by 1975. If they had come before the Khmer Rouge takeover of their country, they were obviously wealthy or influential enough to gain American visas, which was by no means an easy thing for a Cambodian to do. Many from this group of immigrants had previously been in this country either as students, businessmen or government officials.

This first group had an easier path into the employment mainstream of American life than those who came later. For these were the educated, who were more apt to obtain a respectable employment position quickly. This is not to say that the employment they obtained was not a movement downward from what they had known in Cambodia, but it was, none-the-less, a livelihood.

These refugees were also the ones to lay the foundations of Cambodian owned businesses in Long Beach. Today, there are approximately one hundred businesses owned by Cambodians. They are, for the most part, small establishments with an emphasis on food services. There are several restaurants, grocery stores, a couple donut stands, and even a few jewelry stores.

The first group, on the whole, generally came with money. This is the reason many of them were able to open businesses. These businesses, as with the case of the jobs, were generally a step down from what they had known in their native land. It was, however, a means to establish and maintain a comfortable lifestyle.

As the years proceeded, those Cambodians who arrived in Long Beach came directly from refugee camps in Thailand. They were the ones who escaped from their country's forced labor camps and eventual take over by the government of Vietnam. The majority of these people arrived here pre-literate and in a penniless state. Their road into the American job market has been much more difficult.

Upon arrival in Long Beach these refugees are instructed to go through the Refugee Development Program. This, however, now may take several years, for a waiting list has developed. During that time a person is given financial aid or welfare. A family of six currently receives $895.00 per month. Along with this amount the refugees are also provided with aid in obtaining and paying for housing and free medical services. These services are a good deal better than most refugees have ever experienced.

What happens then, as a Cambodian is under the care of the state and waiting for the RDP to begin, is that they develop a dependency on this financial support. If one were to immediately enter the RDP then perhaps they would be less averse to obtaining employment immediately upon its conclusion. What occurs instead, is that the need is planted that there is no need for employment.

There are currently two main agencies, which provide aid to the Cambodians seeking employment once they have completed the RDP. They are the United Cambodian Community and the Cambodian Association of America. These are both private organizations, which obtain funding from the government. The United Cambodian Community last year received in excess of one million dollars. It currently has fifty employees engaged in helping refugees obtain employment.

The United Cambodian Community in 1987 opened a vocational center for refugees and low-income people in what was formerly a garage that they renovated. The initial cost of this project was $700,000.00 and it has met with mixed responses.

Upon completion of the RDP, a Cambodian will go to one of these agencies. This is required by the Welfare Department if the recipient wishes to continue to collect state aid. Once at any agency, the attempt is made to find employment for the refugee.

The United Cambodian Community claims that eight percent of the Cambodians who seek jobs through their agency obtain them. They say only twenty percent fail. This figure is undoubtedly quite altered, for it is known that only thirty percent of the overall Cambodian population of Long Beach is employed. The rest remain on welfare.

The average job that a Cambodian refugee will obtain after completion of the RDP is generally that of a low or no skill position, usually in the manufacturing industry or perhaps in such fields as janitorial or maintenance. They may expect to earn approximately $4.00 per hour. In other words, minimum wage. Due to the fact that they are not illegal aliens and have established agencies behind them, they are never forced to work below minimum wage.

Of the thirty percent that do work, they often have desires for a better job and position. They fully understand that it is they who must strive to learn the language and customs better in order to raise their standing in America. The younger generation of Cambodians who have spent time in the local school system generally have far less of a problem obtaining employment than do their parents. They too realize this is based on their understanding and acceptance of the culture.

As the percentages show, the majority of Cambodian Refugees in Long Beach do not obtain employment. Seventy percent remain under the care of welfare. The reason for this is not hard to see. Within this safe structure all is taken care of: the rent, the food, and any medical expenses. Once one goes off into the job market all aid is discontinued and the individual is forced to assume all responsibilities themselves. The Cambodian agencies have programs set up in order to help the individual make the change from reliance to independence. They help with some of the burden of insurance and rent in the beginning.

It is, of course, not an easy move to make from total support to a world where all things must be paid for by what one earns. In many cases a person with a large family makes more money through the welfare services than they do on the job. For this reason, many remain dependent. In this position they are not required to do much more than they wish within the constraints of their own economic and cultural limitations.

There are twenty-two ways in which one is entitled to continue collecting welfare once they have completed the RDP. Health is the most obvious and most used of these. It is clear that if one is mentally or physically unable to work, they should be excused from it. It is however, the contention of several agencies that many Cambodians complain of false ailments in order that they may remain on welfare.

There are many Vietnamese doctors in nearby communities that are believed to be aiding the Cambodians by writing letters to the effect that they are not physically or mentally able to work, when in fact they are. Periodically the patients must be reexamined. These same doctors are believed to be reconfirming their original false findings. When confronted, the doctors disclaim this fact. The statistics, however, speak for themselves with forty-eight (48) percent of the Cambodian Refugees claiming physical or mental ailments.

From the point of view of health services, The Asian Pacific Mental Health Program has approximately one hundred and twenty-five Cambodians who are seeking psychiatric help due to the traumatic conditions, which they have experienced in their life. Of those who are treated at the program, ninety-four (94) percent are on public assistance, ninety-four (94) percent spoke no English, seventy-six (76) percent are women, seventy-three (73) percent have experienced the loss of a close relative while in Cambodia by murder, torture, or starvation, and forty-six (46) percent were single or widowed. Of those people fifty (50) percent had been tortured and fifty-seven (57) percent had experienced starvation. Of the mental disorders, eighty-five (85) percent were plagued by depression, sixty-four (64) percent had continuing nightmares, and forty-nine (49) percent heard the voices of people who had died.

It is the contention of this organization that many more Cambodians are having delayed stress reactions and emotional and psychological difficulties due to their experiences in Cambodia and their move to the United States than have come forward. It is believed that they do not seek professional help because they either have no conception of the program, and what it does, or they do not understand that they may need psychiatric guidance.

As the conditions that the majority of these people have lived through are horrendous, it can be understood why many of them complain of physical and mental disorders.

It is a continual complaint on the part of refugees that they truly do wish to go out and fend for themselves but they blame their inability on language barriers and lack of skill. It is easy to see their point. It is even clearer that in their pre-literate, uneducated state they cannot, do not, or will not see the adverse effect they are having on the community in which they inhabit. For not only are they taking energy in all forms: monetary, physical, mental, and political, but they are doing nothing to repay the debt nor apparently do they wish to.

No one can argue the point that they, for the most part, did not ask for the war and what happened to their country. One also cannot argue that they are taking advantage of a government that has been kind enough to take them in and allow them the chance for a better life. Few of these Cambodians seem to appreciate their situation. They simply enjoy the harvest without helping to reap the grain.

There is no clear answer for the problem of motivating the Long Beach Cambodians into becoming functional, employed citizens of the community. Each agency has the tendency to blame the other and accuse them of corruption instead of finding an appropriate answer.

If a Cambodian truly wishes to become part of America and not simply biding time until they may hopefully return to their native land, they must make the step to remove themselves from being supported by the American government and move out into the world which they may or may not like, and become a part of it, instead of simply being a burden on it.

Photographs of Businesses in the Cambodian Section of Long Beach, California, circa 1987

Chapter 7
The Politics of Cambodian Refugees in Long Beach, California

Whenever a group of immigrants come to a new country the question of loyalty arises. This is especially true when the people, as in the case of the Cambodian Refugees, come with the attitude that nothing could be worse than what they came from. It was not so much their choice to leave their country, but to leave the conditions that exist within it.

Many Asian groups in the recent past have chosen to immigrate to the United States. Their motives have not only been based on the idea of greater freedom, but that of a better financial future as well. It has been charted that though these Asians choose to come here, their first loyalty is with their native country and secondarily with the United States. Many Americans dislike this fact and feel these people are simply here to experience the economic rewards, and then return to their own country. Though the motives are in question, they are at least understood.

No other group has been forced into making such a choiceless decision of immigration to America than the Cambodians.

Do the Cambodians really choose to be here or would they to prefer to return to their own country if conditions were different? Of those interviewed for this study all but one chose to return to Cambodia if conditions were different. The majority said that if they could, they would return on a permanent basis. They wished for the life they had once known. The other common answer, especially among the younger people, was that they wished to return for visits but preferred to live in the United States where riches were closer at hand.

What ramifications does this hold for America, and specifically, for Long Beach, California? One finds that, to date, there are approximately forty-five thousand Cambodians living in a community and not really contributing to it, while wishing to be elsewhere. This *"Elsewhere,"* is, however, quite impossible to return to on a civilized level.

The alternative for some who wish to return to Cambodia is to join guerrilla groups, which are based in Long Beach. These groups would organize and supply the means in which Cambodians may return and fight Cambodia's former controlling power, the Vietnamese. In other words, here in America mercenaries are gathered and finances collected to wage war on another country.

In America it is unlawful to propagate mercenaries, yet in Long Beach it is known of and apparently overlooked. The United States did not favor the Vietnamese government control of Cambodia. There was, however, no military conflict between the two, except by mercenaries who came out of Long Beach, California.

The main group behind this movement of mercenaries is known as Seiha. This group was formed on 1 August 1976. The name Seiha is the Cambodian word for August, to commemorate their founding. Seiha is supported philosophically and financially by most of the Cambodians in Long Beach. To support this group and the Cambodians who battle as guerrilla soldiers: rallies are held, donations are accepted, and the Cambodian people provided whatever help, in whatever way, they can.

For those Cambodians who wish to return and fight for their country, but are not financially well off, they will return and stay. For the most part, those who return to fight or help medically or otherwise, do so and then come back to Long Beach, returning to their businesses or other employment. Many do this a few times each year. This means that these people have obviously become American citizens or at least registered aliens, due to their ease of travel. The implications of this are obvious. To become an American citizen one is to renounce all alliance to other governments. These people involved in this movement obviously have not.

The former president of the Seiha resistance group, Nil Hul not only owns a business in Long Beach, which has served as Seiha headquarters, but has made an attempt at running for the political office of city council. This is, of course, a very admirable thing. Such actions are needed in a community to bind it together and to try to raise its living standard. The question is where do this man's priorities and loyalties lay with the city or with his return to Cambodia—an obviously desired goal.

On 28 August 1986, Nil Hul was defeated, coming in fourth place with a total of one hundred and fifty-three votes. With the majority of Cambodians either illiterate or non-citizens, this outcome was expected.

As the Vietnamese have now officially left Cambodia, the emphasis of these mercenaries has been placed on which faction of the battling Cambodian political parties they choose to support. This political separation will obviously lead to tensions within the community; because of the fact no figure has stepped forward with enough support to lead Cambodia. Thus, the refugees now no longer have a common force, the Vietnamese, to rally against and will experience political division.

It is an understandable desire that these Cambodians have, of returning to the life they once knew in their native land. They have come up against many barriers here in the United States. It is doubtful however, if these people in the near future, will be able to return to a peaceful Cambodia.

As it has had in the past, Cambodia has many military factions working within it. Not only is the Vietnamese presence still there to a degree but also there are several other groups fighting for political control. These groups include the Khmer Rouge, the Khmer Serei, and others.

The Vietnamese, while at their height, outnumbered the military strength of these groups four to one. Now, with their absence, it is questionable who will emerge victorious. Thus, Cambodia is now expected to enter into another period of civil strife.

There has been political discussion in European countries by all of those who felt they had the support and power to lead Cambodia into a new and more peaceful era. These negotiations however, proved fruitless and only served to separate the warring political groups further, and no political figurehead came from them.

The former King and Prime Minister, Norodom Sihanouk, was the first ousted from power in the current reformation of the Cambodian government in 1970. Though most Cambodians feel he is their King, and though he does hold Cambodia's seat at the United Nations, few feel he could ever reemerge as the country's unchallenged leader. Though the majority of the Cambodian Refugees probably do not want to acknowledge it, there is little hope of the old Cambodia ever returning. Thereby, they are once again forced to make an influenced decision and try to be Americans. Though their desire to return is admirable and all the energy placed in the movements gives them hope, it is that same energy and hope that removes them from functioning in America.

Of those surveyed for this study, more than half were, or wished to become, citizens of the United States if they could not return to Cambodia. Several were not even sure what it meant to be a citizen.

Most were curious if it would affect their welfare benefits.

To the traditional Cambodians, government is not for the people. It is something far and separate from the average person, though most do have their political views. In Cambodia most of these predominately preliterate peasant farmers never even heard of the concept of voting people into public office. Thus, only approximately three thousand of the refugees are registered to vote here in the United States and attempt to take part in their local community.

The Cambodians of Long Beach make up the largest percentage of Indo-Chinese Refugees in the city. They are also the fastest growing community. New arrivals come often, not only from refugee camps in Thailand, but also from other American cities. This rapidly growing number must be given attention by not only the City of Long Beach, but by higher governmental branches as well. The question arises that with all this energy being poured into these people, will they ever be Americans, free willingly, or will they simply become a further burden on this society wishing only to return to their native land whenever possible?

Chapter 8
Cambodian Assimilation
of American Culture

The percentage or amount of assimilation that a new ethnic group has obtained in a new culture is not an easy determination to make. There are many variants and factors that must be taken into consideration to determine this. Not only is the ability to function in the culture brought up, but also is happiness and self-fulfillment.

The first criterion that must be considered when analyzing this; is there a need? It has been found with many new immigrant groups, that if there is no need to move outwards, the people will simply stay within their own ethnic minority. This has been especially true in the case of female immigrants who, for the most part, were not required to earn a living; thus only frequented the places where the native language was spoken and customs observed. The male immigrants, on the other hand, have been the predominant financial support of the family. They have had to move away from the indigenous group and out into the new society in order to support the family.

In the Cambodian community of Long Beach, we have seen that there are a high percentage of those who have no need to move beyond their own ethnic and cultural group. This has been due to the fact that they have been offered financial support by the government. Neither the female nor the male Cambodians find it necessary for survival to force them to accept and learn the new culture and language in order to find employment and thereby, make a living for themselves. They have chosen the alternative route of simply accepting their fate and living within its bounds.

Can the system that allows one to have little or no need to assimilate be questioned? This is a philosophic issue. For in the Cambodian community there have been those, few in overall numbers, who have made the choice to move outwards in society at all costs. Were these people simply better equipped to do so, or was it individual desire and need? These questions, in truth, can never be answered, for each individual case is unique. All that can be understood is the factors that have led to the conditions of assimilation, or non-assimilation, such as it may be.

To understand the assimilation patterns, the Cambodians who now live in Long Beach must be broken up into three groups. The first are that of the first wave of immigrants who came to this country during the mid-seventies or earlier. The second are the second wave of refugees who arrived in the late seventies and eighties. The third group is the children of these refugees who are either currently attending school or have recently completed it.

The first group of Cambodians who arrived here were, as mentioned earlier in this study, those of the elite families of Cambodia. They were predominantly the educated, the wealthy, and political officials. When they arrived here they had at least a vague understanding of western culture and its attributes. Once here, they chose to raise their position and standing in this society, as they had done in their own. One must be aware that these were the people who were obviously successful in their own country.

Can one then make the observation, as stereotypical as it may be, that these people were the self-motivated and aggressive ones of their society? This, when put to the test, seems to be a very obvious conclusion, even when the consideration of the previous generation's initial financial support was involved. This group of incoming Cambodians is the ones who have worked their way up and have gained fruitful employment and have aggressively assimilated, or at least tolerated, the American culture.

This first group was the ones to lay the foundation for the next wave of Cambodians who immigrated here. This first group aided in softening the blow of culture shock for this second group. However, in doing this, they undoubtedly also aided in making these people a group bound by dependency.

As the movement of post Khmer Rouge peoples began to come, they were led to the Long Beach area in hopes of contact with other Cambodian people and the promise of United States government aid in the forms of education, medical, and financial. Once they arrived in Long Beach they were informed of the requirement of education through the Refugee Development Program. As they became involved in the program they realized that the American culture was hard to understand and accept. Upon completion of the RDP these people simply fell back into a much easier and more desirable position of dependency. The attempt at education and forced assimilation proposed by this program, simply failed.

It is true that the majority of the second wave immigrants were peasants. They also were not of the motivated and educated breed of the first Cambodians to arrive. Never-the-less, beyond the point of the required Refugee Development Program (RDP), most have made no attempt in assimilating American culture.

The ability for this second group to move forward has been available. Many who arrived post 1979, which were of the educated of Cambodia, now have good positions and are financially independent. Can this be solely attributed to lifestyles in the past? To see this issue clearly one must realize that there have been large numbers of immigrants, legal and otherwise, who have entered the United States in recent years who, even though they did not speak the language nor completely understand the culture, have found ways in which to come to support themselves within this society and often times live in better conditions than those of the Cambodians of Long Beach.

The conclusion must be made that it is not simply the motivation or education of the first group that sets them apart from the assimilation patterns of the second. It is the desire. A group of people may sit around and discuss and debate how bad their conditions are and do little to change them.

It is quite undoubted that there is much frustration in the lives of the Cambodians. What is even clearer is that if they chose to live here on American soil, they must find the desire within themselves to assimilate the culture and move forward into American society. They cannot simply dream of returning to Cambodia.

The first group of Cambodians who came to Long Beach meant well and began to set up organizations in which to help their fleeing countrymen. In this process, they somehow have accomplished just the opposite. For though these organizations help in many ways they do more to keep the people bound by their own inabilities and ignorance than they do to aid in assimilation.

There has also been an effort by cultural and religious organizations to make the Cambodians feel more closely linked to their home. There has been a traditional Cambodian dance school set up in Long Beach. A Cambodian Christian church exists in Long Beach and a Cambodian Buddhist temple that was first located in a home in nearby Lakewood, California, purchased with a loan and individual donations of fifty dollars ($50.00) each. It then moved to a much larger former union hall location in Long Beach at the cost of one million, one hundred thousand dollars ($1,100,000.00)— also purchased with donations and a loan. These facilities aid in keeping Cambodians, especially the younger ones, in touch with their cultural heritage. It is debated if they aid in assimilation rather than simply increase the cultural barriers.

The third and final group of Cambodian Refugees that must be viewed to understand assimilation trends is the younger generation. These are the ones who either arrived in the United States at an early age or were born in the United States. Children, of course, have a better ability of acceptance than do adults. These young people have attended public schools and have put time and energy, whether willingly or otherwise, into assimilation. These young people have at least the best understanding of American culture and will, in time, come to be the most functional parts of it.

The parents of these children are the first to criticize the new ideas and morals presented by their offspring. They feel that their children are losing their cultural heritage. This is true, at least to a certain degree, for the young people have the ability to adapt and accept new ways. A better way for the parents to feel, perhaps, is that their children are becoming a better part of the culture in which they now live.

In all cases of movement, from one culture to another, there is the loss and gain effect. If one holds too tightly to the culture from which they have come, they rob themselves of truly experiencing the new one. A balance must be found of keeping the Cambodian culture and accepting the American.

At times it appears that those who have assimilated American culture to a degree have taken on more of the bad patterns of American life, than that of the good ones. For last year, sixty Cambodians were arrested for drunk driving—these people coming from a culture where drinking is considered a sin.

The conclusions that are reached in studying the three groups of Cambodian immigrants and their ability to assimilate American culture is that, the first have assimilated and become part of the American culture at least to an acceptable degree. The second group, on the whole, has either the unwillingness, lack of desire, or inability to become a true functional part of this society in the near future. The third group, the young refugees, have come to the highest functional level of all three groups of Cambodians and will, in the future, have a great deal to offer the United States.

Chapter 9
Survey

There were two surveys conducted for this study of Cambodian Refugees in Long Beach, California to gain information that was not revealed elsewhere, in previous studies. This survey was designed to uncover the most important factors of the community without being threatening to those questioned. Though the survey is quantitative in nature and quantitative theory, by its very definition has much room for variation and deviation, it is believed that the results of these two surveys reveal a true picture of the community.

The first survey was taken of one hundred Cambodian Refugees and was conducted in August of 1986. Of the one hundred surveys conducted, ten were done of students at Long Beach City College; ten were done of Cambodian business owners or Cambodian business employees. The remaining eighty were done door-to-door in the Cambodian section of Long Beach.

The second survey was completed in June of 1989. One thousand Cambodian

Refugees were interviewed, completely on a door-to-door basis.

The first and second surveys, though three years apart in their execution, reveal almost the exact same outcome and answers. What does this show us? That little progress or change has taken place, in Long Beach, California, over this period of time.

Chapter 10
Sample Survey of Cambodians in Long Beach, California

I. General:

    1) Male or Female
    2) Age (approximate)
    3) Married or single
    4) Any children
    5) Number of

II. English level:

    0 = None
    1 = Basic
    2 = Intermediate
    3 = Advanced
    4 = Excellent

III. Cambodia:

    6) Educational level of Cambodia?
    7) Occupation of Cambodia?
    8) Reason for leaving Cambodia?
    9) How long were you in refugee
        camp?
    10) Means to the U.S.:

    A. Sponsor
    B. Family
    C. Other

IV. United States:

    11) First relocation city?
    12) If not Long Beach, why did you
        relocate to Long Beach?
    13) Do you wish to live in the U.S. or
        Cambodia?

    Why?

    14) Are you a U.S. citizen?
    15) Do you wish to become a U.S.
        citizen?

V. Occupation:

    16) Occupation in the U.S.
        A. Like
        B. Dislike

    17) What occupation would you
        desire?

VI. Refugee Development Program:

    18) Did you attend RDP?

19) Did you learn English in the U.S. or Cambodia?

20) Were you trained for a job in RDP

    A. What?

21) Did you obtain that job?

    B. Why?

22) Do you desire more RDP?

    If yes
    A. More time?
    B. More training?

23) Does RDP help?

VII. Welfare:

    24) Do you prefer being on welfare or working?

    A. Why

VIII. Education:

    25) What subject interests?
    26) Will you continue to college level?

27) Will you continue to university level?
28) What occupation do you wish to obtain?
29) Did your parents attend a college or university?

      If Yes:
      A. U.S.?
      B. Cambodia?

IX. Housing:

30) Household type:

      A. House?
      B. Apartment?
      C. Other?

31) Size?
32) Number of people living there?
33) Do you wish to stay in current living situation?
34) Do you wish to remain living with your family?

X. Comments:

35) Things you are most unhappy
    with in the U.S.?
36) Things you are most happy with
    in the U.S.?

_____*Chapter* **11**

Survey Results of One Hundred
Cambodian Refugees in Long Beach, California
Completed in August 1986

I. General:

    1) Male or Female?

        53   Female

        47   Male

    2) Age (approximate)

        Age span   13 – 62

        Median   24.5

        Average   34

    3) Married or Single?

        72 married

        28 unmarried

    4) Any Children?

        Of 72 married

        71 had children

        Of 28 unmarried

        4 had children

        All widowed or unknown location of spouse.

5) Number of Children?

       Children span 1 – 9

       Median   4

       Average   4

II. English level:

0 = none

1 = basic

2 = intermediate

3 = advanced

4 = excellent

       21 at level 0

       27 at level 1

       32 at level 2

       11 at level 3

        9 at level 4

III. Cambodia

6) Educational level in Cambodia?

       26 None

       49 Less than 8 years

       19 More than 8 years

        6   University level

Note: some were below the age to have been expected to receive schooling in Cambodia.

7) Occupation in Cambodia?
- 69 Farming
- 2 Fishermen
- 3 Construction
- 1 Mechanic
- 1 Businessman
- 2 Military officers
- 1 School teacher
- 2 Government officers
- 2 University students
- 17 Children

8) Reason for leaving Cambodia?
- 100 Political conditions

9) How long were you in refugee camp?
- Span: 3 months to 32 months
- Median: 14.5 months
- Average: 13 months

10) Means to the U.S.?
- 76 Refugee/sponsor
- 22 Family
- 2 Other (both obtained direct visa)

IV. United States
11) First relocation city in U.S.?
- 54 Long Beach
- 46 Other

12) If not Long Beach,
    why did you relocate to
        Long Beach?
    20 Came for Cambodian
        community.
    12 Came due to educational
        opportunities.
    3   Came for warmer weather.
    1   Came for employment
        opportunities.
    10 Did not like original
        relocation city.

13) Do you wish to return to
    Cambodia?
    99 Yes
    1   No

14) Are you a U.S. citizen?
    20 Yes
    80 No

15) Do you wish to become a U.S.
    citizen?
    31 Yes
    20 No
    29 Unknown

V. Occupation:

16) Occupation in the U.S.?
71   None
2   Business owner
7   Food service employee
3   Factory worker
16   Students

A. Like?
B. Dislike?
64   Like
46   Dislike

17) If unhappy; what occupation
would you like?
19   Any work
12   Own business
10   Advanced labor
5   Office

VI. Refugee Development Program
18) Did you attend RDP?
62   Yes
10   Currently attending
14   No
14   Waiting

19) Did you learn English in the U.S.
    or Cambodia?
    9   Some English in Cambodia
    91   In U.S. or no English
         spoken

20) Were you trained for a job in
    RDP?
    *Of the 62 who have completed
         the program:*
    58   Yes
    4   No

         A. What occupation?
              15   Plumbing
               2   Auto repair
               7   Sewing
               1   Nursing
              12   Electrical
              13   Carpentry
               7   Too young to
                   receive
                   training.

21) Did you obtain that job?
    58   No

    A. Why?
         34   Medical incapability
         17   Not available

1   Job (nursing)
Made them sick.
1 Found another job
1 No reason

22) Does the RDP need to be longer?
    59 Yes
    3   No

    A. More time?
        62 Yes
        0   No
    B. More English?
        62 Yes
        0   No
    C. More job training?
        52 Yes
        10 No

23) Does RDP help?
Of the 72 who have or are attending:
72 Yes
0 No

VII. Welfare:
    24) Do you prefer being on welfare?
    Of the 71 unemployed:
    64 Yes
    7 No

Of the 13 who are employed:
3 Yes
9 No

A. Of the yes, why?
  48 America is hard to
    understand
  9 Wages not high
    enough.
  6 Expenses too high
    without welfare
  7 Unknown

VIII. Education:
  25) What subject interests?
    16 students, all with interests in
    Business and Management

  26) Will you continue to college
    level?

    *Of the six public school
    students:*
    2 Yes
    3 Unknown
    1 Students currently attending
    Long Beach City College.

  27) Will you continue to university
    level?
    Of the 10 college students:

2 Yes

6 Unknown

28) What occupation do you wish to
obtain?
4 Business owner
6 Business worker
6 Unknown

29) Did your parents attend a college
or a university?
2   Yes (in Cambodia)
15 No

IX. Housing:
30) Household type?
31 House
68 Apartment
1   Business

31) Size?
All houses two or more
bedrooms

Apartments:
18 Two bedrooms
26 One bedrooms
24 Singles

32) Number of people living there?

Houses:
Span   4 – 20
Average 14

Apartments:
Two bedrooms:
span   6 – 13
average 9

One bedroom:
span   5 – 16
average 9

Singles:
span   5 – 11
average 5

Business:
Of the business surveyed, the owner admitted living there with eight others inhabiting the same structure.

33) Do you wish to stay in your current living situation?
    70   Yes
    22   No
     9   Undecided

34) Do you wish to remain living with your family?

84 Yes

16 No or maybe

X. Comments

    35) Things you are most unhappy
        with in U.S.?

        64 Language problem

        21 Cultural problems

        13 Financial problems

        2 No comment

    36) Things you are most happy with
        in the U.S.?

        17 Opportunities

        19 Freedom

        14 Education

        7 Financial areas

        43 Unknown

Chapter 12

Survey Results of One Thousand Cambodian Refugees in Long Beach, California

Completed in June of 1989

I. General:

    1) Male of Female?

        642   Female

        358   Male

    2) Age (approximate)

        Age span 6 – 79

        Median 45.5

        Average 41

    3) Married or single?

        593 Married

        407 Unmarried

    4) Any children?

        of 593 married 591 had children of 407 unmarried 159 had children

        All widowed or unknown location of spouse.

5) Number of children
Span 1 – 14
Median   7
Average   5

II. English level:

0 = None
1 = Basic
2 = Intermediate
3 = Advanced
4 = Excellent

328 at level 0
204 at level 1
232 at level 2
156 at level 3
80 at level 4

III. Cambodia

6) Educational level in Cambodia

401 – None
541 – Less than 8 years
34 – 8 years or more
4 – University level

Note: Some were not born or below the age to have been expected to receive education in Cambodia. Twelve of those who attended universities did so in other countries, including the U.S. and France.

7) Occupation in Cambodia?
- 519 Farming
- 81 Fishermen
- 4 Mechanics
- 31 Businessman
- 51 Military
- 2 School teacher
- 1 Government officers
- 14 University students
- 236 Children or not born
- 61 Housewives

8) Reason for leaving Cambodia?
All for political conditions, except for the two that were born in the United States.

9) How long were you in refugee camp?
Span: 1 month to 39 months
Median: 19.5 months
Average: 14 months

10) Means to the U.S.?
Refugee 642
Sponsor 311
Family 34
Visa 11

IV. United States
11) First relocation city in U.S.?
441 Long Beach
559 other

12) If not Long Beach,
Why did you relocate to Long Beach?
297 Cambodian community
8 Educational opportunities
56 Warmer weather
8 Employment opportunities
143 Did not like original relocation city
47 No reason

13) Do you wish to return to Cambodia?
976 Yes
24 No

14) Are you a U.S. citizen?
107 Yes
893 No

15) Do you wish to become a U.S.
     citizen?
     182   Yes
     542   No
     169   Unknown

V. Occupation:
     16) Occupation in the U.S.
          701   None
           63   Business owner
           27   Food service employee
           60   Worker
          149   Students

               A. Like?
               B. Dislike?
                  349   Like
                  651   Dislike

     17) What would you like to do (if
          unhappy)?
          182   Any work
          198   Own business
          100   Advanced labor
           62   Office
          109   Undecided

VI. Refugee Development Program
    18) Did you attend RDP?
        581 Yes
        112 Currently attending
        183 No
        124 Waiting
    19) Did you learn English here or in
        Cambodia?
        14 Some English in
             Cambodia
        986 In U.S. or no English
             spoken

    20) Were you trained for a job in
        RDP?
        of 581 who have completed
        program
        564 Yes
         17 No

        A. What?
            186 Plumbing
             68 Auto repair
             59 Sewing
              8 Nursing
            156 Electrical
             84 Carpentry
              3 Too young to
                 receive
                 training

21) Did you obtain that job?
  13 Yes
  551 No

   A. Why?
     321 Medical
        incapability
     97 Job not
       available
     1 Job (nursing)
      made them sick
     18 Found another
      job
     110 No reason

22) Does the RDP need to be longer?
  461 Yes
  120 No
   A. More time?
    579 Yes
    1 No
   B. More English?
    581 Yes
    0 No
   C. More job training?
    564 Yes
    17 No

23) Does RDP help?

Of 581 who attended:

579 Yes

   2 No

VII. Welfare:

24) Do you prefer being on welfare?

Of the 701 unemployed

598 Yes

103 No

Of the 150 who are employed

92 Yes

58 No

   A. Of the yes, why?

163 America hard to
     understand

189 Wages not high enough

292 Expenses too high
     without welfare

46 Unknown

VIII. Education:

25) What subject interests?

of 149 students

137 in Business and
     Management

2 in medicine

2 in politics

6 in law

26) Will you continue to college level?
Of the 89 public school students
69   Yes
20   Unknown

27) Will you continue to university level?
Of the 58 college students
5   Yes
50   Unknown
2   Currently at university level

28) What occupation do you wish to obtain?
127   Business owner
11   Business person
2   Doctor
1   Nurse
5   Lawyer
1   Politician

29) Did your parents attend a college or university?
18   Yes
130   No

IX. Housing:
    30) Household type?
        197   House
        785   Apartment
        18   Business

    31) Size?
    All houses two or more
    bedrooms

    Apartments:
        142   Two bedrooms
        541   One bedroom
        102   Singles

    32) Number of people living in?
    Houses:
        Span 2 – 20
        Average 9

    Apartments:
    Two bedrooms,
        Span   5 – 15+
        Average 9

    One bedroom,
        Span   2 – 16
        Average 8

Singles,

> Span   3 – 11
> Average   5

Business,

> Of the eighteen businesses surveyed, the owners of four admitted living there with other family members. It was obvious in three other locations that they too lived on the premises.

33) Do you wish to stay in your current living situation?

> 654   Yes
> 297   No
> 49   Undecided

34) Do you wish to remain living with your family?

> 826   Yes
> 174   No or maybe

X. Comments

35) Things you are most unhappy with in U.S.?

> 318   Language problem
> 421   Cultural problems
> 163   Financial problems

98   No comment

36) Things you are most happy with
   in U.S.?
   51   Opportunities
   451   Freedom
   200   Education
   171   Financial areas
   127   Unknown

Survey Illustrations

Illustration 2
Level of English
Survey Results

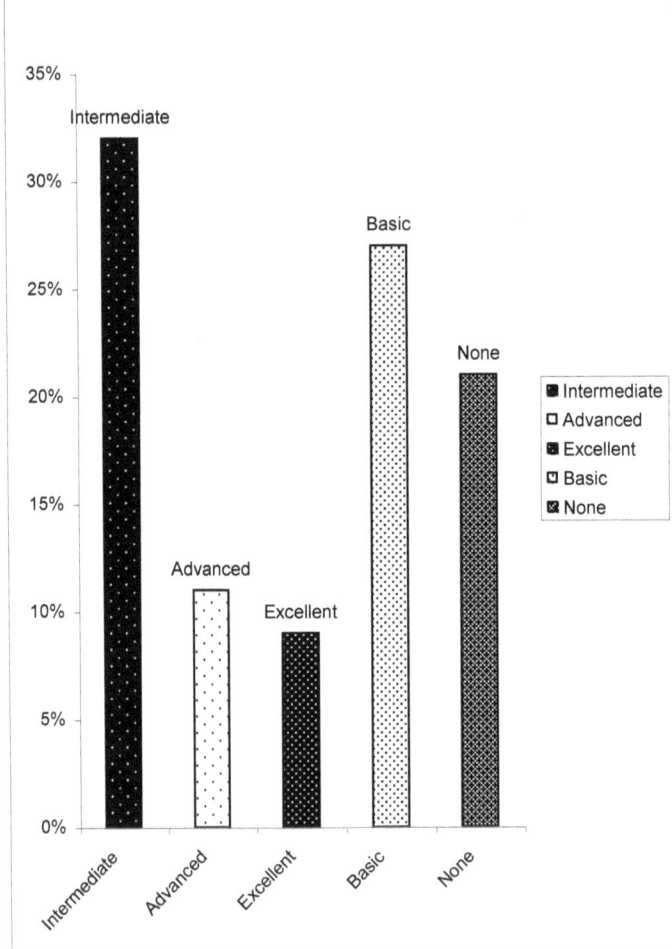

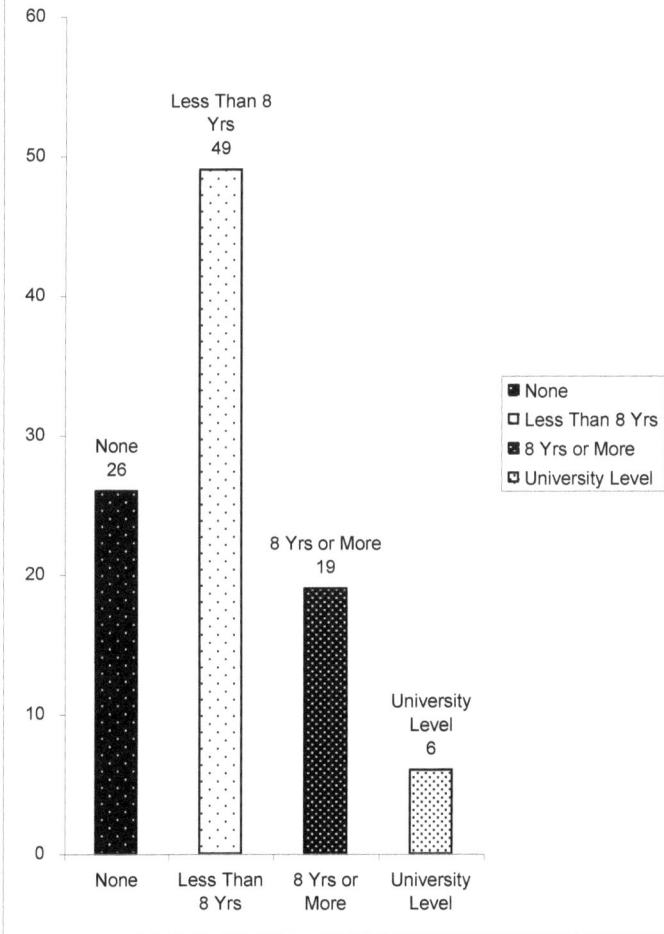

Illustration 3
Educational Level
Survey Results

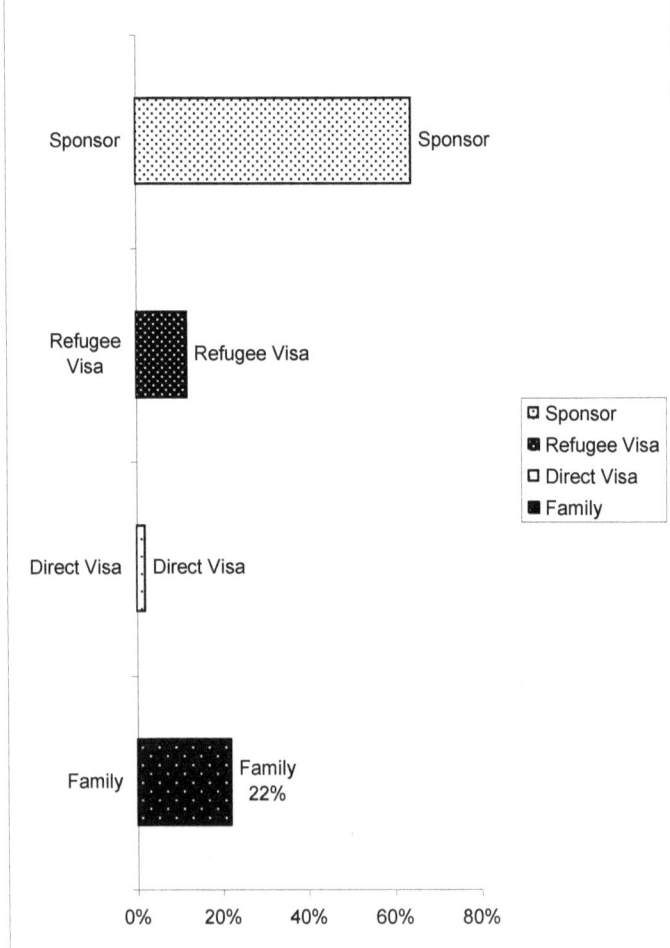

Illustration 4
Means to the U.S.
Survery Results

122

Illustration 5
Desire for Cambodian Return
Survery Results

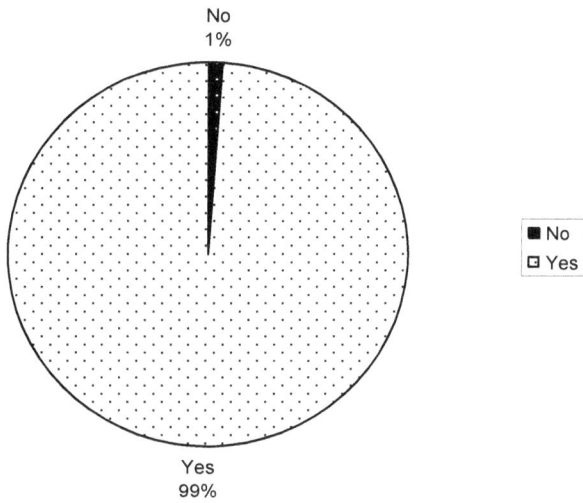

No
1%

Yes
99%

No
Yes

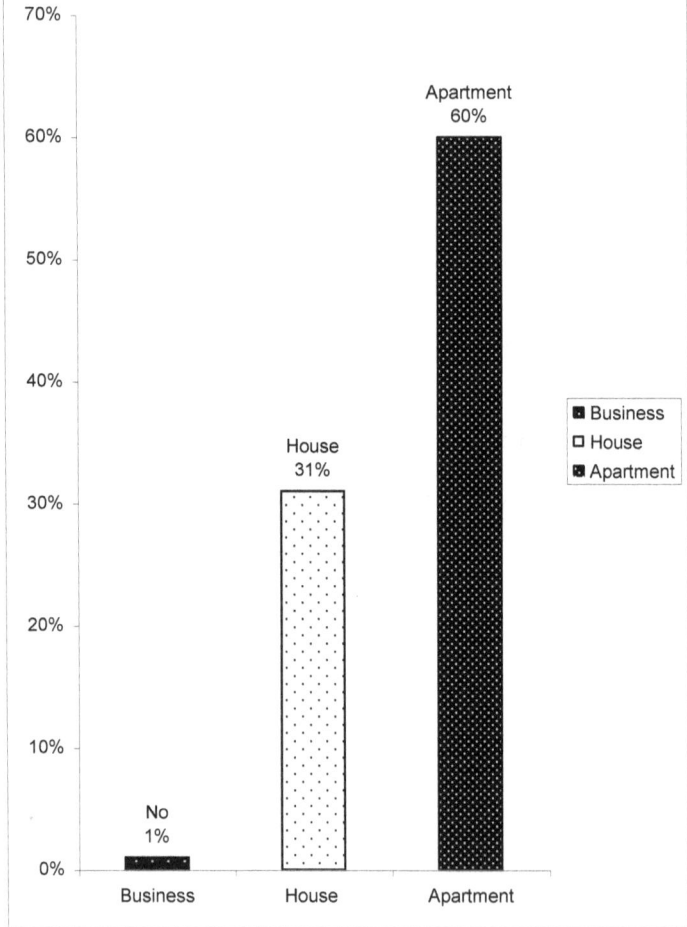

Illustration 6
Household Types
Survey Results

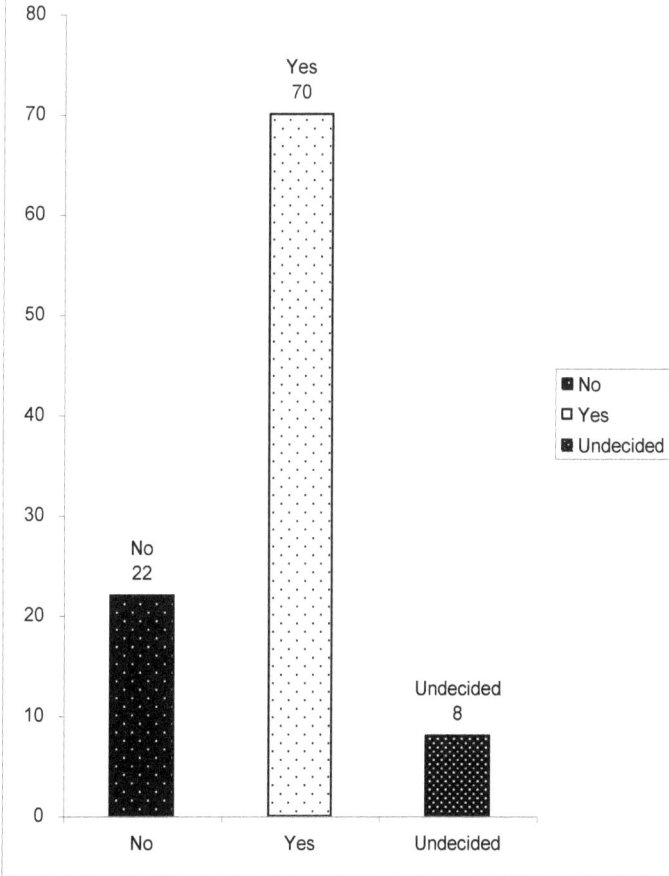

Illustration 7
Housing Contentment
Desire to Remain
Survery Results

Illustration 8
Desire to Live With Family
Desire to Remain
Survey Results

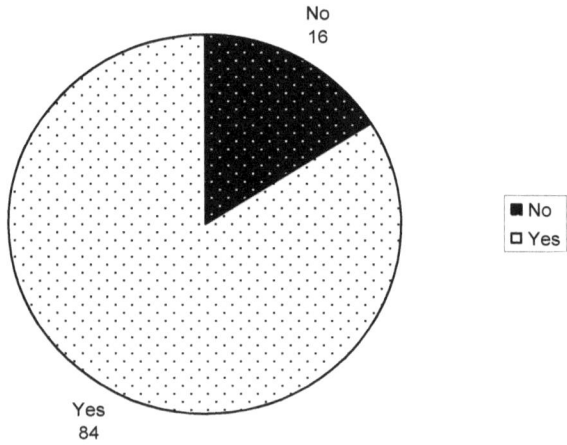

No
16

Yes
84

■ No
□ Yes

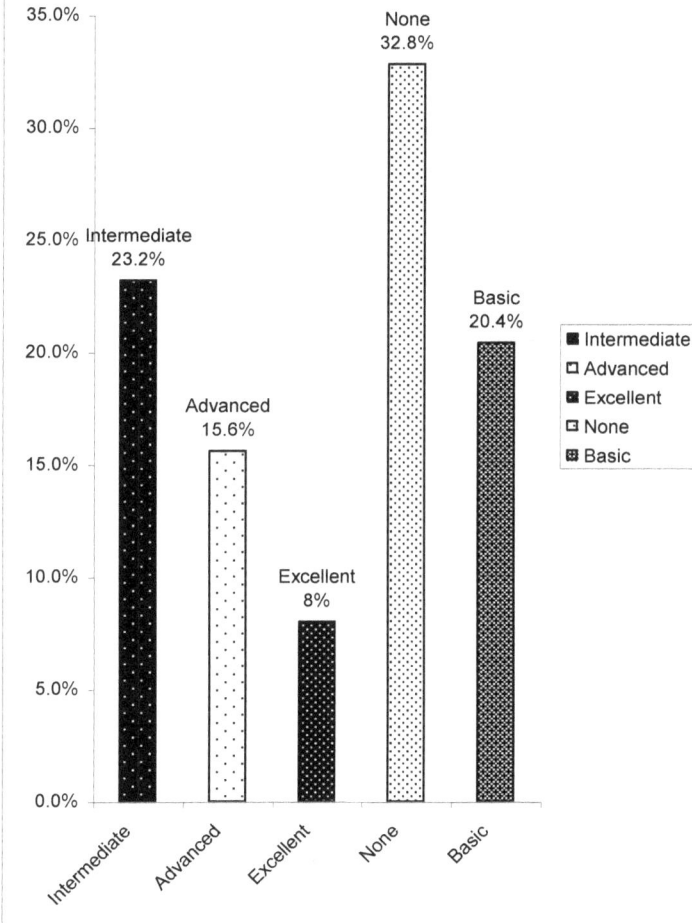

Illustration 9
Level of English
Survery Results

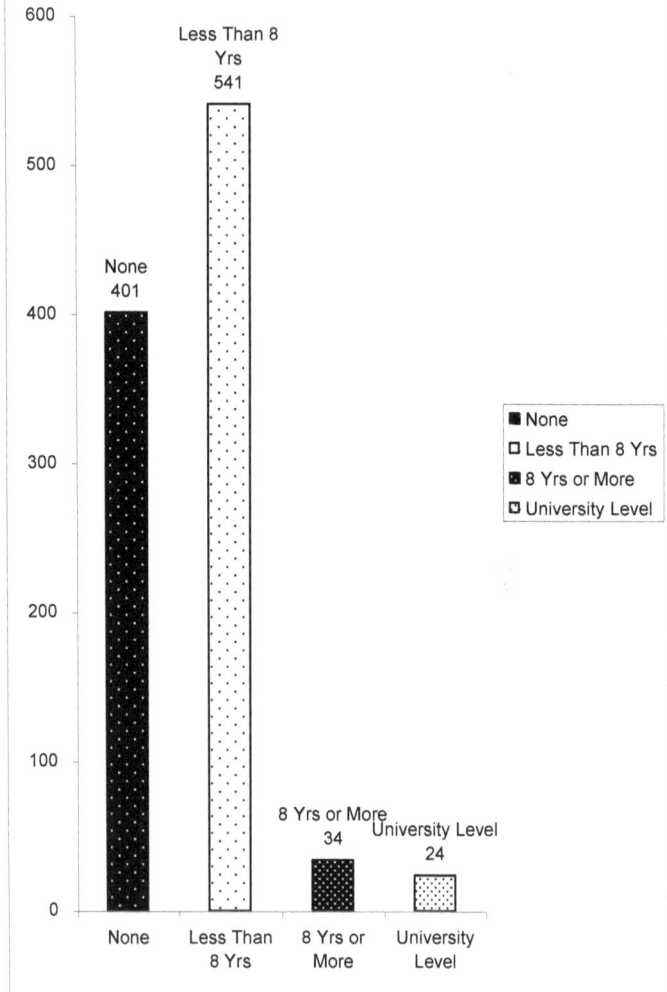

Illustration 10
Educational Level
Survery Results

128

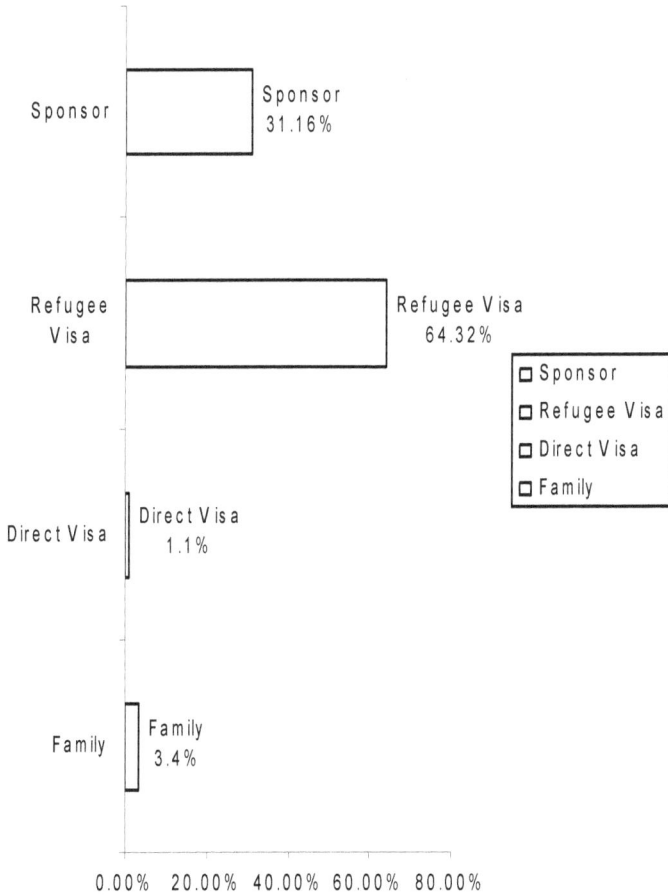

Illustration 11
Means to the U.S.
Survery Results

Sponsor — Sponsor 31.16%

Refugee Visa — Refugee Visa 64.32%

Direct Visa — Direct Visa 1.1%

Family — Family 3.4%

Legend:
□ Sponsor
□ Refugee Visa
□ Direct Visa
□ Family

0.00% 20.00% 40.00% 60.00% 80.00%

129

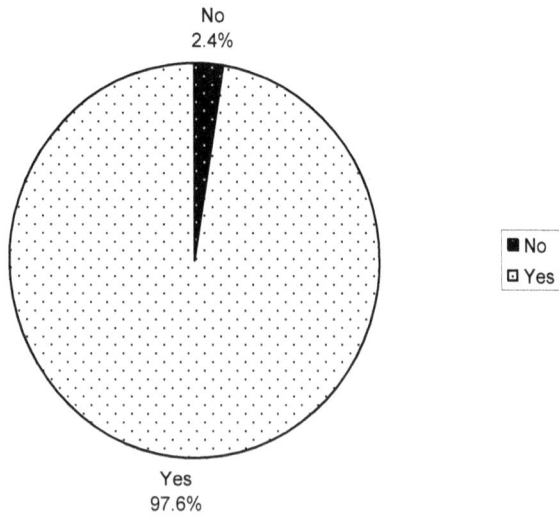

Illustration 12
Desire for Cambodian Return
Survery Results

No
2.4%

No
Yes

Yes
97.6%

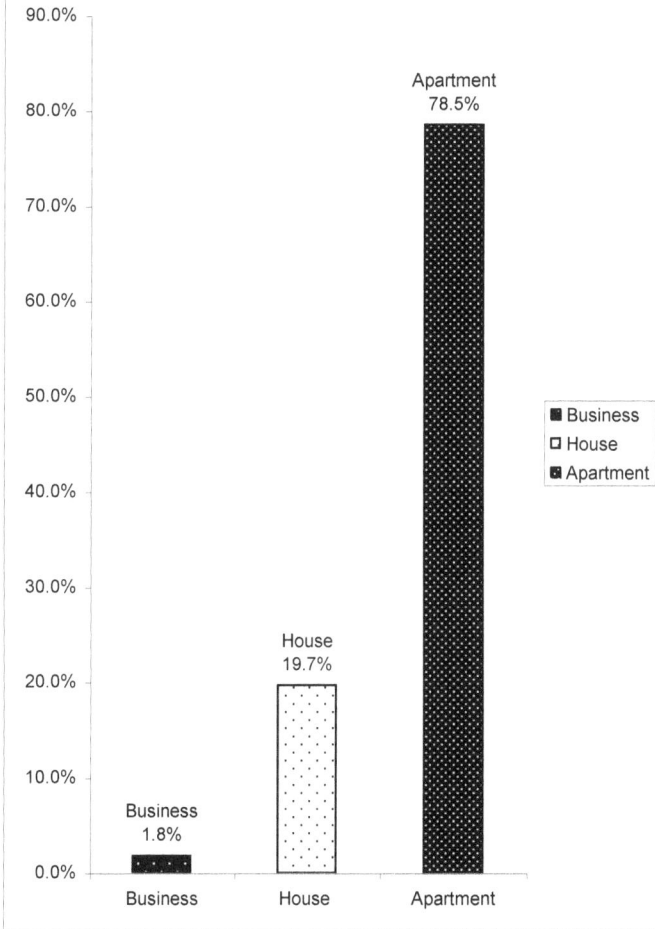

Illustration 13
Household Types
Survey Results

Business 1.8%

House 19.7%

Apartment 78.5%

Legend:
- Business
- House
- Apartment

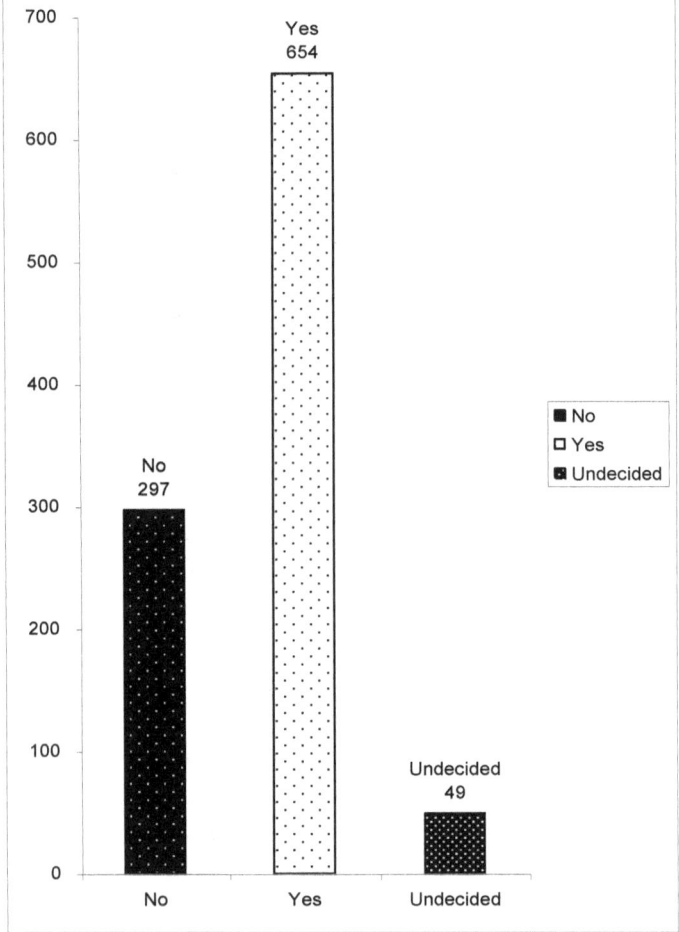

Illustration 14
Housing Contentment
Survery Results

Illustration 15
Desire to Live with Family
Survery Results

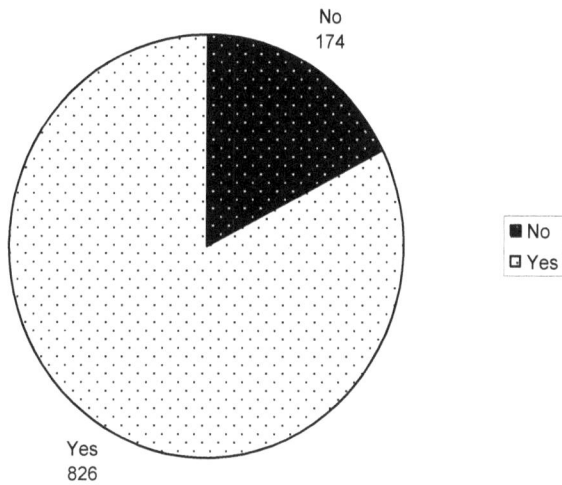

No
174

Yes
826

- No
- Yes

134

Conclusion

Through this study, it has been learned that the Cambodians who have come to the United States have done so to escape the political conditions of their native Cambodia. Upon arrival, here in America, most have made all haste to relocate to Long Beach, California. The city of Long Beach has had, due to this massive influx of a new ethnic group, a worsening urban condition and has had to recently reevaluate its understanding of the problem and what appropriate actions must be taken.

The Cambodians, which reside in this area, known as *Phnom Penh by the Sea,* are hopelessly locked into the syndrome of dependency on the government for support. Though these Cambodians have gone through a reeducation program, most have had little opportunity to move away from their state of dependency and become a functioning part of American society.

The Cambodians who reside in Long Beach made the choice, as influenced as the decision was, to relocate to the United States. Once here, their dreams and expectations have not been fulfilled and now most of them desire to return to their native

Cambodia. What Long Beach is left with is an ethnic group of newly arrived refugees who do not and cannot assimilate the culture and wish simply to return to their homeland if political conditions were different.

Long Beach and the Cambodian community are left with little hope of impending change. The community will continue to grow. It will not only be fueled by new refugees, but by arriving family members, and those relocating from other parts of the United States. The City of Long Beach and the State of California need to analyze what motivating factors may be put into application in order to get the community to move outwards and into the American mainstream. The Cambodians who inhabit the area would do more for themselves and the city if they were to place returning to Cambodia in the back of their minds and put all efforts into American assimilation.

References

Armstrong, John P. Sihanouk Speaks. New York: Walker and Company, 1964

Burchett, Wilfred. Norodom Sihanouk, My War with the CIA. New York: Pantheon Books, 1973

Burchett, Wilfred. The China Cambodia Vietnam Triangle. Chicago: Vangaurd Books, 1981

Caldwell, Malcolm and Tan, Lek Hur. Cambodia in the Southeast Asian War. New York: Monthly Review Press, 1973

Cambodian Mutual Assistance Associations Project. Executive Summary of Workshop Held at the Second National Meeting of the Cambodian Cluster Project. Long Beach, 1981

Chandler, David P. A History of Cambodia. Boulder: Westview Press, 1983

Chandler, David P. and Kiernan, Ben., eds. Revolution and its Aftermath in Kampuchea: Eight Essays. New Haven: Yale University Southeast Asia Studies Monograph Series No. 25, 1983

Etcheson, Craig. The Rise and Demise of Democratic Kampuchea. Boulder: Westview Press, 1984

Espenshade, Edward B., ed. Goode's World Atlas. Chicago: Rand McNally and Company, 1982

Institute of Asian Studies. Thailand's Policy Towards the Vietnam-Kampuchea Conflict. Bangkok: Chulaongkorn University Asian Studies Monographs No. 032, 1985

Kiljunen, Kimmo. Kampuchea Decade of the Genocide. London: Zed Books 1984

Kulke, Hermann. The Devaraja Cult. Ithaca: Cornell University Southeast Asia Program Data Paper number 108, 1978

Leites, Nathan. The Vietcong Style of Politics. Santa Monica: Prepared for the Office of the Assistant Secretary of Defense by the Rand Corporation, 1969

Los Angeles County Commission on Human Relations. The New Asian Peril. "Report of a Hearing on Rising Anti-Asian Bigotry." Los Angeles, 1984

Los Angeles County Commission on Human Relations. Plight of the New Americans: Discrimination Against Immigrants and Refugees. Los Angeles, 1985

Mazzeo, Donatella and Antonini, Chiara Silvi. Monuments of Civilization Ancient Cambodia. New York: Grosset and Dunlap, 1978

Munson, Frederick P., team chairman, Area Handbook for Cambodia. Washington D.C.: U.S. Government Printing Office, 1963

Munson, Frederick P. Area Handbook for Cambodia. Washington D.C.: U.S. Government Printing Office, 1968

Ngor, Haing. A Cambodian Odyssey. New York: Macmillan Publishing Company, 1987

Nixon, Richard. The Real War. New York: Warner Books, 1989

Osborn, Milton. Before Kampuchea. Sydney: George, Allen and Unwin, 1979

Ponchaud, Francois. Cambodias Year Zero. New York: Holt, Reinhart and Winston, 1977

Robinson, H. Monsoon Asia. Estover: MacDonald and Evans LTD, 1978

Samphan, Khieu. Cambodia's Economic and Industrian Development. Ithaca: Cornell University Press, 1979

Smith, Rodger M. Cambodias Foreign Policy. Ithaca: Cornell University Press, 1965

Sharan, Mahesh Kumar. Studies in Sanskrit Inscriptions of Ancient Cambodia. New Delhi: Abhinau Publications, 1974

Shawcross, William. Sideshow Kissinger, Nixon and the Destruction of Cambodia. New York: Simon and Schuster, 1979

Shawcross, William. The Quality of Mercy. New York: Simon and Schuster, 1984

Steinberg, David J. Cambodia its People its Society its Culture. New Haven: HRAF Press, 1957

Tang, Truong Nhu. A Vietcong Memoir. San Diego; Harcourt Brace Jovanovich, Publishers, 1985

United States Census, 1970

United States Census, 1980

United States Census, 1986 update

United States Census, 1989 update

Vickery, Michael. Cambodia 1975 – 1982. Boston: South End Press, 1984

Whitaker, Donald P. Area Handbook for the Khmer Republic (Cambodia). Washington D.C.: U.S. Government Printing Office, 1973

Zasloff, Joseph J. Kampuchea: A Question of Survival. Hanover: American University Staff Reports No. 47. 1980

About the Author

Scott Shaw, Ph.D. is uniquely qualified to assess the Asian immigration patterns in the United States. He possesses a doctorate in Asian Studies, is a native of Los Angeles, California, and has since a young age been directly involved with the study and experience of Eastern Thought. He continually returns to Asia, documenting obscure aspects of Asian culture in words and on film. He is the author of numerous works on Asian Studies, Zen Buddhism, Yoga, and the Martial Arts. These books have been translated in numerous languages and are available around the world.

Scott Shaw's *Books-In-Print* include:

About Peace:
    A 108 Ways to Be At Peace
    When Things Are Out of Control
Advanced Taekwondo
Chi Kung for Beginners
Essence: The Zen of Everything
Hapkido: Essays on Self-Defense
Hapkido: The Korean Art of Self Defense
Independent Filmmaking:
    Secrets of the Craft
Marguerite Duras and Charles Bukowski:
    The Yin and Yang
    of Modern Erotic Literature
Mastering Health: The A to Z of Chi Kung
Nirvana in a Nutshell
Samurai Zen
Taekwondo Basics
The Ki Process:
    Korean Secrets for
    Cultivating Dynamic Energy
The Little Book of Yoga Breathing
The Little Book of Zen Mediation
The Tao of Self Defense
The Warrior is Silent:
    Martial Arts and the Spiritual Path
Yoga: The Spiritual Aspects
Zen Buddhism:
    The Pathway to Nirvana
Zen Filmmaking

Zen in the Blink of an Eye
Zen O'clock: Time to Be